Hunting Gear

Annie Wendt Hemstock

PowerKiDS press™

New York

Open Season

Published in 2015 by The Rosen Publishing Group, Inc.
29 East 21st Street, New York, NY 10010

First Edition

Editor: Amelie von Zumbusch
Book Design: Greg Tucker
Book Layout: Joe Carney
Photo Research: Katie Stryker

Photo Credits: Cover Dave Blackey/All Canada Photos/Getty Images; p. 4 RubberBall Productions/Vetta/Getty Images; p. 5 Werner Forman/Universal Images Group/Getty Images; p. 6 Hans Huber/Getty Images; pp. 7, 11 Jupiterimages/Stockbyte/Thinkstock; p. 9 Design Pics/Thinkstock; p. 13 Thinkstock/Stockbyte/Thinkstock; p. 15 Gilles_Paire/iStock /Thinkstock; p. 17 Shane Thompson/iStock/Thinkstock; p. 18 Pierdelune/iStock/Thinkstock; p. 19 Volodymyr Burdiak/Shutterstock.com; p. 21 FooTToo/iStock/Thinkstock; p. 23 Rene Kohut/Shutterstock.com; p. 25 Jeanne Hatch/iStock/Thinkstock; p. 26 GuySagi/Hemera /Thinkstock; pp. 27, 29 Steve Oehlenschlager/Shutterstock.com.

Library of Congress Cataloging-in-Publication Data

Hemstock, Annie Wendt, author.
 Hunting gear / by Annie Wendt Hemstock. — 1st ed.
    pages cm. — (Open season)
 Includes index.
 ISBN 978-1-4777-6730-6 (library binding) — ISBN 978-1-4777-6731-3 (pbk.) —
ISBN 978-1-4777-6732-0 (6-pack)
 1. Hunting—Juvenile literature. 2. Hunting—Equipment and supplies—Juvenile literature.
 I. Title.
 SK35.H425 2015
 799.2028—dc23
                              2014004217

Manufactured in the United States of America

CPSIA Compliance Information: Batch #WS14PK3: For Further Information contact Rosen Publishing, New York, New York at 1-800-237-9932

Contents

Gear Up!

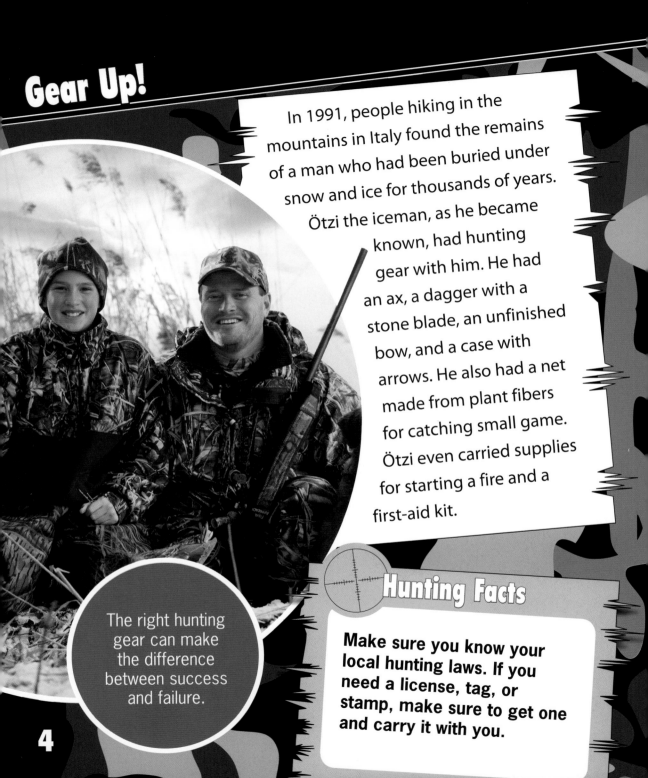

In 1991, people hiking in the mountains in Italy found the remains of a man who had been buried under snow and ice for thousands of years. Ötzi the iceman, as he became known, had hunting gear with him. He had an ax, a dagger with a stone blade, an unfinished bow, and a case with arrows. He also had a net made from plant fibers for catching small game. Ötzi even carried supplies for starting a fire and a first-aid kit.

The right hunting gear can make the difference between success and failure.

Hunting Facts

Make sure you know your local hunting laws. If you need a license, tag, or stamp, make sure to get one and carry it with you.

Ancient cave paintings like this one tell us that human beings have used hunting gear for thousands of years.

Hunters today have many kinds of gear available. We do not have to sew our own hunting clothes or make our own arrows. We do not have to melt lead to make our own bullets. Let's look at some of today's gear that can help us be successful hunters.

If you are out hunting or scouting, you need to be ready if something goes wrong. Carry your gear in a comfortable pack. Bring water and food, like energy bars or jerky. Lightweight rain gear, gloves or mittens, a hat, and extra socks will keep you dry and warm. A map and **compass** or a GPS will help you find your way.

Building a fire is not as easy as it looks! If your hunt involves camping, make sure you know how to build and put out a fire safely.

Hunting Facts

It takes skill to use a GPS or to read a map and compass. Make sure you know how to use your gear before you set out on a hunting trip with it.

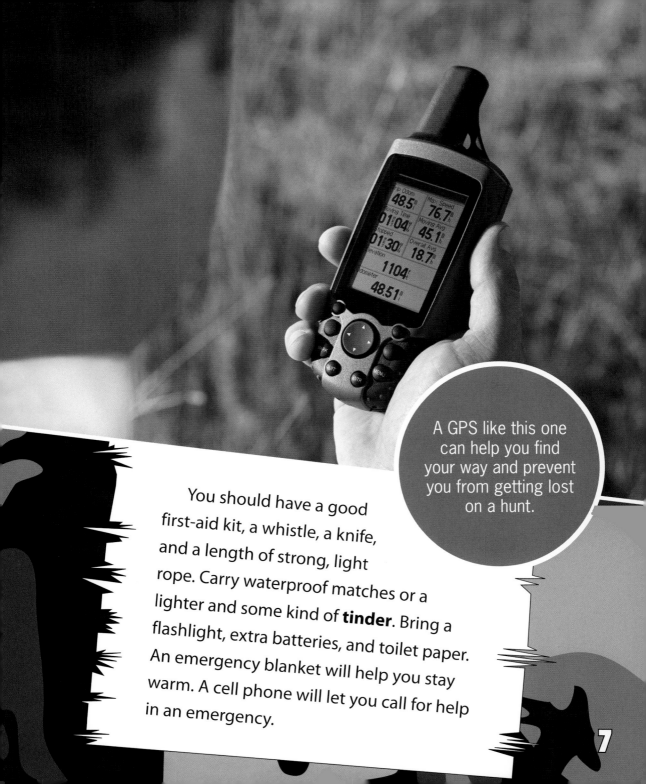

A GPS like this one can help you find your way and prevent you from getting lost on a hunt.

You should have a good first-aid kit, a whistle, a knife, and a length of strong, light rope. Carry waterproof matches or a lighter and some kind of **tinder**. Bring a flashlight, extra batteries, and toilet paper. An emergency blanket will help you stay warm. A cell phone will let you call for help in an emergency.

Dress for Success

When you head out to hunt, it is important to pick the right clothes. If your hands are cold, it will be harder to make that good shot when the time comes. If you get wet, you might get so cold that you could end up in serious trouble.

There are many kinds of hunting clothes. Some of them have **camouflage** patterns that help you blend in with what is around you. You can find clothes that look like bark, leaves, cattails, and snow.

Hunters wear camouflage to hunt some animals, such as waterfowl. It helps them blend in with their surroundings.

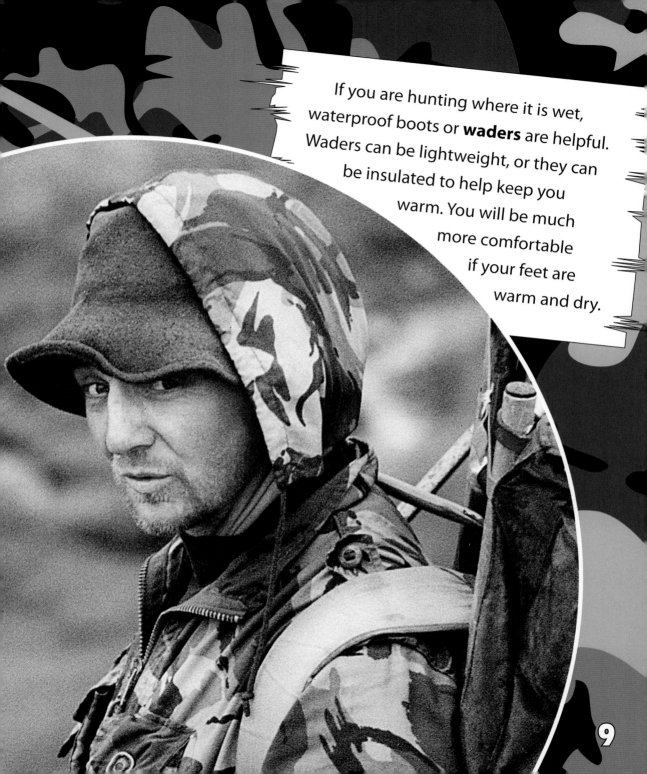

If you are hunting where it is wet, waterproof boots or **waders** are helpful. Waders can be lightweight, or they can be insulated to help keep you warm. You will be much more comfortable if your feet are warm and dry.

For some kinds of hunting, you are required to wear hunter, or blaze, orange. Hunter orange is easy to see because it is very bright. Many animals, such as deer, have eyes that are different from ours. Their eyes are good at seeing when there is very little light. They do not see colors the way we do. Hunter orange does not look bright to them. They notice movement more than colors.

When you are wearing hunter orange, other hunters can see you more easily. Hunters are sometimes required by law to wear hunter orange. Many hunters wear hunter orange even when they do not have to. They know that it is safer to be seen by other hunters.

This hunter wears a blaze orange jacket so other hunters can spot her and will not shoot in her direction. Many states require big-game and upland-bird hunters to wear blaze orange.

Choose Your Weapon

Rifles are the first choice for many kinds of game. They are designed to shoot one bullet at a time. Rifles are very accurate and can shoot a long distance. Rifles come in different **calibers**. You will want to pick a caliber that will have enough power to make a good, clean kill. The .22-caliber rifle is a good choice for small game, such as squirrels. Larger-caliber rifles, like a .270 or a .30-30, are better for big game, such as deer.

Rifle ammunition is called a cartridge. Using a rifle or cartridge that is too powerful can cause too much damage and waste meat. There are charts that can help you pick the right rifle and ammunition for your **quarry**.

This hunter aims a rifle. Rifles shoot farther than any other hunting firearm. They are best for big game.

Look at your gun's barrel. You will find a data stamp that tells you the right kind of cartridge or shell for that gun. Make sure your ammunition matches the data stamp.

Shotguns are designed to shoot many small pellets at a time. The pellets spread out as they leave the gun barrel. The pellets do not travel as far as a rifle bullet. This means you must get closer to your quarry.

Shotguns come in different **gauges**. Shotgun ammunition is called a shell. Inside the shell are the gunpowder and the pellets, or shot. Small shot is used for game birds and small animals. Larger shot is used for hunting geese or turkeys. A single, heavy shot, called a slug, is used for hunting deer. There are charts to help you pick the right gauge and shot size for the animals that you plan to hunt.

This shotgun is ready to be loaded. The shells are packed with many small pellets called shot.

A Bow in the Hand

Bows and crossbows are ancient weapons. Longbows and recurve bows are the simplest kinds of bows. Compound bows have cables and **cams** that make them easier to draw and hold back the string.

Arrows used to be made of wood. Each arrow would be a little different from the other arrows. Modern arrows are made from aluminum or carbon. They are stronger and more **consistent**. Make sure your arrows are matched to your bow. Crossbow arrows are often called bolts.

This young hunter draws back his bow and takes aim. He is ready to shoot.

Bow hunters today can choose from many different kinds of arrowheads. Broadheads have metal blades that are very sharp. Field points are used for practice but can also be used for hunting small game. Blunt points are designed to stun small animals.

Finding your quarry can be a challenge. Animals can be hard to see at a distance. Luckily, we do not always have to rely on our own eyes. A good pair of **binoculars** can make things look bigger. They can help you be sure of your target before you raise your weapon.

Binoculars and scopes can help you see animals from far away. A close-up view of this deer shows it is young and has no antlers.

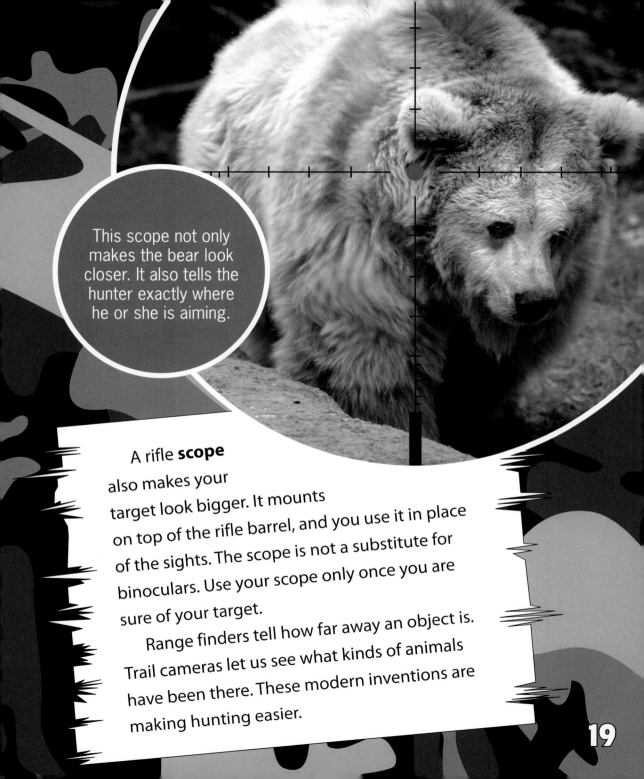

This scope not only makes the bear look closer. It also tells the hunter exactly where he or she is aiming.

A rifle **scope** also makes your target look bigger. It mounts on top of the rifle barrel, and you use it in place of the sights. The scope is not a substitute for binoculars. Use your scope only once you are sure of your target.

Range finders tell how far away an object is. Trail cameras let us see what kinds of animals have been there. These modern inventions are making hunting easier.

Game animals are **wary**. In order to survive, they are alert to danger. Hunters try to avoid being noticed. If you can stay hidden, animals might get close enough for you to take a good shot.

Tree stands let you sit or stand up off the ground. Many animals, like deer and bears, do not expect danger from overhead. A hunter in a tree stand must be very still and quiet to keep from being detected.

There are several styles of blinds. Elevated blinds like this one are sometimes called tree stands.

Blinds are something that you can use to hide from your quarry. Some blinds are short screens made of cattails or other plants. Others are little rooms put up on poles. There are blinds that look like camouflaged tents. Blinds keep animals from seeing you move.

Hunting Facts

If you hunt from a tree stand, always use a safety harness. Many hunters have been hurt falling from their stands.

Getting Closer

Animals will rarely get close if they do not feel safe. Hunters use decoys to make their quarry feel safe enough to come close. Decoys generally look like the animals you are hunting. Sometimes, they look so real you might think they are alive.

Most hunters have seen waterfowl decoys. There are decoys that look like both male and female turkeys. Rabbit, squirrel, and fawn decoys are used for luring predators such as coyotes. Even a feather dangling from a stick can be a decoy.

Good decoys can fool game animals. They can also fool other hunters. Always take care when you place decoys.

Always be careful when using decoys. Other hunters might not know that you are using decoys. They may shoot at a decoy thinking that it is a live animal. If you are behind the decoy, you could be hit by mistake.

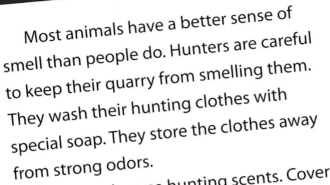

Most animals have a better sense of smell than people do. Hunters are careful to keep their quarry from smelling them. They wash their hunting clothes with special soap. They store the clothes away from strong odors.

Hunters also use hunting scents. Cover scents smell like things in nature, such as pine trees, dirt, or other animals. These scents help mask your human smell. Lure scents smell like things that attract your quarry. They may smell like food or another animal of the same **species**. Using scents can bring animals closer.

An elk calls to his herd. A good elk call fools an elk by sounding exactly like another elk.

Hunters use calls to imitate animal sounds. With practice, you can learn to sound just like your quarry. You can use calls to bring animals closer. Predators can be lured by the sounds of their prey or an injured animal.

25

Handle with Care

When you go hunting, be prepared to **dress** any animals you take. A sharp knife is the most important tool for dressing your kill. You should bring a sharpening tool in case your knife gets dull. Bring string or cord to tie off the bladder and intestines. Keep the meat clean of hair, dirt, and insects. If you take care of the meat, it will taste better and be less likely to spoil. Fabric game bags protect the meat but still allow it to cool quickly. They come in many different sizes.

Carrying out the meat can be hard work, especially if you are hunting big game. A rope, pack frame, sled, or wheeled carrier can help you bring your meat out of the woods.

Always bring a sharp knife to field dress your game. Otherwise, the meat will be ruined.

Hunting Facts

Make sure you follow the laws about tagging and registering game. You may have to bring your animal out of the woods before dressing it.

You should always think ahead about how you plan to carry the quarry you shot home.

A Look to the Future

The right hunting gear can help you be a successful hunter. Today's weapons are accurate. Lures, scents, and decoys bring game closer. Technology makes it easier to find game. Camouflaged clothing and blinds keep hunters hidden.

How will gear get better in the future? People are making smart guns with computers inside that help you make long shots. They are making bullets that guide themselves to the target. New fabrics will keep you warm and dry without being bulky. Maybe one day, we will even have the technology to become invisible!

This young hunter brought the right gear on his hunt and was successful.

Some people like the challenge of hunting the traditional ways. Others enjoy using all the latest gadgets. Either way, there is gear to help you be successful on your next hunt.

Happy Hunting

- ⊕ Know how to use your gear. Practice at home until you are comfortable with it.
- ⊕ Make sure your gear is in good shape before you go hunting.
- ⊕ If your gear pack is comfortable, you will be less likely to leave it at home.
- ⊕ Practice survival skills so that you will know what to do if there is trouble.
- ⊕ Know the laws before you go hunting.
- ⊕ Always tell someone where you are going and when you will be back.
- ⊕ Always handle a gun as if it were loaded.
- ⊕ Keep your finger away from the trigger until you are ready to shoot.
- ⊕ Make sure you know what is in front of and behind your target.
- ⊕ When you are dressing your kill, wear hunter orange so other hunters can see you.

Glossary

binoculars (bih-NAH-kyuh-lurz) Handheld lenses that make things seem closer.

calibers (KA-luh-berz) Measurements of how wide gun openings are.

camouflage (KA-muh-flahj) Having a pattern that matches its surroundings.

cams (KAMZ) Spinning or sliding parts that make a compound bow easier to draw.

compass (KUM-pus) A tool made up of a freely turning magnetic needle that tells which direction is north.

consistent (kun-SIS-tent) Done the same way every time.

dress (DRES) To gut, or remove an animal's inner organs.

gauges (GAYJ-ez) Measures of how wide the barrel of a gun is.

quarry (KWOR-ee) Something that is being hunted.

scope (SKOHP) A metal tube with lenses inside that a hunter looks through to make a target look larger.

species (SPEE-sheez) A single kind of living thing. All people are one species.

tinder (TIN-der) Things that burn easily and can be used to light a fire.

waders (WAY-derz) Pants or overalls worn to walk through water.

wary (WER-ee) Careful and on the watch for danger.

Index

A
animal(s), 10, 14, 17–25, 26
arrow(s), 4–5, 16

B
binoculars, 18–19
blade(s), 4, 17
bow(s), 4, 16
bullet(s), 5, 12, 14, 28

C
case, 4, 26
clothes, 5, 8, 24

D
dagger, 4

F
first-aid kit, 4, 7

G
game, 4, 12, 17, 26, 28
gauge(s), 14

K
kind(s), 4, 7, 8, 10, 12–13,
    16–17, 19

L
lead, 5

O
Ötzi the iceman, 4

P
pack, 6, 30

Q
quarry, 12, 14, 18, 21–22,
    24–25

S
scope, 19
snow, 4, 8

T
tinder, 7

W
waders, 9

Websites

Due to the changing nature of Internet links, PowerKids Press has developed an online list of websites related to the subject of this book. This site is updated regularly. Please use this link to access the list: www.powerkidslinks.com/os/gear/